ESSENTIAL GUIDE TO MAKING SALES
Unlocking a new model of selling

Alvin G. Taylor

INTRODUCTION

Over the years, the way businesses sell their products or services has evolved significantly. With the advent of technology and the widespread use of the internet, the traditional models of selling have given way to newer, more innovative models. One such model that has gained popularity in recent years is the "new model of selling."

The new model of selling is based on the concept of providing value to customers and building long-term relationships with them. Instead of focusing solely on closing a sale, businesses using this model prioritize building a rapport with their customers and providing them with the information and resources they need to make informed purchasing decisions.

One of the key features of the new model of selling is the use of technology to streamline the sales process. By leveraging automation tools, businesses can automate routine tasks, such as lead generation, lead nurturing, and follow-up, allowing sales teams to focus on higher-value activities, such as building relationships and providing value to customers.

Another important aspect of the new model of selling is the emphasis on creating personalized experiences for customers. By leveraging data and analytics, businesses can better understand their customers' needs and preferences, and tailor their sales strategies accordingly. This not only improves the customer experience but also increases the likelihood of closing a sale.

Finally, the new model of selling is characterized by a collaborative approach to sales. Instead of siloed teams and departments, businesses using this model emphasize cross-functional collaboration, bringing together marketing, sales, and customer service teams to create a cohesive customer experience.

Overall, the new model of selling represents a significant shift in the way businesses approach sales. By prioritizing customer value, leveraging technology, creating personalized experiences, and promoting collaboration, businesses can build stronger, more profitable relationships with their customers, ultimately leading to increased sales and revenue.

Table of content

CHAPTER 1

The New Sales Approach

Due to changes in customer behavior, new business models, and technology improvements, numerous new selling methods have evolved in recent years. Some of the most notable ones are listed below:

Customers in a subscription-based business pay a regular price for access to a good or service. Software firms and content providers who provide a monthly or yearly membership frequently employ this.

Freemium model: This model combines components of a subscription-based business model with those of the conventional sales model. Customers can use a basic version of a product or service for free under this model, but they must pay to use the premium features.

Influencer-driven sales: With the popularity of social media, businesses are increasingly using influencer marketing to connect with potential clients. Influencers help brands market their goods and increase sales through paid postings, reviews, and endorsements.

Direct-to-consumer (D2C) sales: This business model entails selling goods to customers directly rather than through conventional retail channels. This is made feasible by the internet and e-commerce platforms, which let businesses skip conventional distribution routes and reach a worldwide audience.

Sales powered by artificial intelligence: As AI technology develops, some businesses are utilizing chatbots and virtual assistants that are AI-powered to engage with clients, give product information and execute sales transactions.

Instead of disrupting potential consumers with pushy sales pitches, inbound selling focuses on attracting and enticing them with valuable information and other resources.

Customer-centric approach: The new selling paradigm emphasizes getting to know the customer and learning about their needs rather than just trying to seal a deal.

Data-driven insights: With the abundance of data at their disposal, sales teams can now leverage data and analytics to better understand their clients and focus their marketing efforts.

Multi-channel strategy: Consumers want to interact with businesses on their terms, therefore sales staff must be able to do the same. These channels include email, social media, and live chat.

What Is Necessary

Any sales model has a shelf life due to shifting business needs and the emergence of new purchasing channels thanks to technology. Similar to the life cycle of a product, customers often start out as generalists and then develop more specialized tastes. Customers have more options and can place higher demands on suppliers in terms of product performance and quality when products change and new competitors enter the market. Businesses lose an advantage when they don't change their sales model to reflect shifting customer wants and behavior.

The most crucial way businesses react to market changes is by creating a relevant sales model that everyone can comprehend, from C-suite executives to field salespeople. The sales model is made up of three main parts:

1. Selection criteria for customers.
Any business strategy and sales model must make choices about where to concentrate your sales force inside a market. When time is wasted on the wrong goals, sales costs rise and the market is left open to competition. The effectiveness of your company's capacity to

implement the plan is directly impacted by sales call patterns—where salespeople spend their time and which opportunities they chase. Are their efforts concentrated on the right-sized accounts, the type of consumers the firm needs in the future, and striking a balance between acquiring new clients and keeping existing ones?

Top leaders are aware that you cannot please everyone. Yet, there is a misalignment between the sales models for the products and services and what they can achieve for particular clients. More often than not, the customer profiles of businesses include reactive answers to customers approaching them rather than a deliberate effort to connect with the ideal businesses.

Sales managers frequently tell their team members to "go forth and multiply," either outright in meetings or inferentially through reward plans. To meet their sales targets, salespeople respond to these demands by selling to everyone, frequently at a discount. Loss of profitability and weakened brand positioning result from this.

Clarity regarding the ideal clients and demographics that the business needs for its present and future growth is necessary for profitable growth.

The cost of sales and account mix based on the company's strategy are two important areas Sales Focus Advisory emphasizes as part of the sales improvement assessments. The overarching trend is that businesses are overstaffed and carrying excessive sales expenditures while concentrating on legacy sales strategies as opposed to what will be needed in the future. But if properly focused, the sales unit frequently has enough bandwidth to produce over 40% growth without adding personnel or spending more money.

Significant growth can be made, and the client base can be shifted to match the company's goals by focusing on the correct targets and aligning with the necessary sales strategy. business planning. A shift in management approach is frequently necessary and gives CEOs more transparency.

On the other hand, a sales leader's ability to define a business plan is one of the fundamental prerequisites for effective customer selection, as no sales model can compensate for a weak business model.

2. Describe your clients and their purchasing procedure.
What buyers want from a product and what they want from it varies widely. While some customers prefer digital or virtual sales methods that embrace distant selling, others want face-to-face interactions between field sales and decision-makers. To maintain a competitive

advantage, sales models must adapt to incorporate the various kinds of B2B buying, which is no longer a single process.

Businesses need to stay in touch with their clients and customers to avoid applying outdated theories about why people buy things or forming their own opinions about what those reasons might be. Instead, they must detail which issues

In a recent project, the lack of growth in the company affected a typical manufacturing industry. The company had chosen a voice for the market that was out of step with the buyers, even though the products were sound and had a stellar reputation, and the gap was widening as the market continued to evolve.

Through marketing communications and sales dialogues, the topic was altered, resulting in the development of a new sales model. Salespeople were now better able to answer questions and persuade customers as a result of the modification. The result was a large rise in business and an improvement in the caliber of customers approaching the organization.

Looking at new measures for managing sales teams is a business concept.

3. The economics and go-to-market metrics
After examining more than 200 businesses, it was shown that the time salespeople spend connecting with consumers is a crucial component of all growth. Normally, they spend only 25–30% of their time doing this, which creates significant room for improvement. The amount of time salespeople spend on various tasks is a critical factor in your capacity for growth. Their ability to sell longer has a direct impact on the achievement of sales revenue.

The widely used "Wins" measure is used by many businesses to monitor sales performance. The issue is that salesperson activity is directly related to the number of wins (and losses). Wins and defeats can be undermined by a lack of activity.

Another lagger metric wins. It is the process's culmination, whereas the process's beginning must place attention on the activity and its goal. Analytics on conversions only help when they are tracked throughout the entire process, not just at the conclusion.

To maximize sales effectiveness, consideration should also be paid to the product's pricing, shipping, and technical reliability. Sales of a product that is not competitive with other products on the market will still occur, but not at the same rates as those opportunities that are available and being captured by your rivals.

4. Rebuilding the sales force
Effective salespeople are masters in comprehending their industry and the businesses

of their clients, and they should act as consultants capable of providing reliable advice. If your B2B sales team doesn't fit that description, you'll need to re-enable them so they can have such interactions.

Selling brings buyers and sellers together in a cooperative process. The buyer is not helped when a product is forced upon a person or business that is not ready. It won't create the proper customer connection for a lasting relationship, word-of-mouth recommendations, and maximum revenue.

If your salesperson says, "That's not how we work...," that is another red flag. They probably haven't considered how much the world has changed and may yet change; instead, they are saying, "We have tried all this before, let's keep doing what we know."

You can be sure that everything around your industry has changed even if you work in one where the changes are less visible. The globe is evolving in terms of the need for communication, information collecting, decision-making procedures, and cooperation among various providers to produce project acquisitions. Every industry is impacted by how the world runs, and supply chains have changed.

The sales manager must guarantee that the appropriate interactions and targeting are taking place in the market. The early transparency that

CRMs provide for customer interactions, targeting, and deal movement is crucial.

Sales leaders must confirm their early findings by being on-site.
By paying attention to what is being said, challenging your team's thinking with the proper questions, and ensuring they have access to the right resources and information, you can help them be more productive.

CHAPTER 2

The Most Significant Issues In Sales

Nowadays, a sales representative's ability to clinch a deal depends more on the potential customer than it does on their skills. The availability of technology has made consumers more knowledgeable than ever.

Before making a choice, they can do research about the business, the products, and even the salespeople. They are knowledgeable about what will work for them, can compare your proposal to all of your competitors, and will not be persuaded by a cold call.

In reality, most customers make their purchasing decisions before even speaking with a sales representative.

Before contacting you, your prospect has most likely whittled down their list of potential providers to two or three.

Successful salespeople are beginning to abandon their outdated hard-sell techniques and transition into a "trusted advisor" role as Inbound Marketing matures.

Sales representatives must interact with clients on their chosen channels to stay on top of the rapidly changing consumer sentiments, which are today greatly impacted by technology. Also, they must be genuine and supportive in their attitude and messaging.

Businesses must include these shifting attitudes in their sales strategy.

15 sales problems sales representatives face

1. Developing online trust
2. Integration of the marketing and sales teams
3. Receiving feedback from potential customers
4. Sealing deals
5. Finding quality prospects
6. Involving numerous corporate decision-makers
7. Refraining from discounting 8. Phone contact (getting in touch)
9. Making use of social media in the selling process
10. CRM tools
11. Making a point of urgency
12. Addressing concerns about price

Lead management, qualification, nurturing of unprepared leads, upselling, and returning business

These are the top challenges faced by sales reps:

1. Developing online trust
The majority of sales representatives today primarily communicate with their prospects via phone calls and emails as a result of the Covid-19 global epidemic and social distance protocols. This has its own set of difficulties because it can be difficult to stand out from the various emails and phone calls that potential clients receive. It takes fresh strategies to set yourself apart from your rivals while creating a virtual barrier between you and your prospects.

Personalized interactions can be used to accomplish this. It is essential to have a "human" salesperson who the prospect can relate to and connect with during the sales engagement. To meet the prospect on their terms, you must also make sure that your efforts are timely, relevant, and on the appropriate platform.

2. Integration of the marketing and sales teams
The conventional separation of sales and marketing can harm lead management and, ultimately, your ability to close business. Duplication and loss of data are nearly certain to happen when marketing and sales work in separate systems and manage data separately.

Solution: To combat this, sales and marketing teams must shatter barriers of convention and collaborate as an integrated system of objectives and procedures. This can be accomplished by integrating both teams and the leads/prospects they are working on into a central hub of truth (consolidated, consistent data).

3. Receiving feedback from potential clients

The majority of sales representatives concur that getting a response from prospects is their biggest problem. Consumers are less receptive than ever despite the abundance of devices and communication capabilities at our disposal. This can be the result of an abundance of channels or just information overload.

Sales representatives must stand out from the competition and develop into dependable consultants in the eyes of their clients.

Use video to set yourself out as a solution. Include a video in your email to get in touch with leads. It's known as "video prospecting." You may do this using programs like HubSpot, Loom, and Vidyard.

4. Sealing of deals

The second most difficult part of selling is closing a sale. People throughout the world are experiencing difficult economic circumstances, and in a market that is becoming more competitive, consumers don't want to feel pressured into making purchases.

Instead, modern buyers favor doing the research themselves. Search engines and other widely available tools make it simple to learn everything there is to know about a business, a product or service, or even a sales representative.

The salesman must become thoroughly aware of the difficulties that their potential customer faces to tailor a solution to meet their needs.

Answer: What inquiry do your potential customers frequently pose to you? We all have that one question that people ask us and we all have the perfect response. If someone asks you a question, record a video of your response and post it to a blog. You only need a smartphone to complete this. Put the information on your company blog and spread it widely on LinkedIn and other social media. You may do so once more each month! Do not be timid.

5. Finding quality prospects
Finding quality leads is getting more and more difficult. The leads that salespeople receive from their companies are generally of very low quality, which is one of the main concerns we hear from them.

Consumers may easily interact with brands and businesses, but how do salespeople identify the good deals from the bad? The solution is in the alignment of the sales and marketing departments, with an SLA in place.

marketing and sales sla

Using a strong CRM that can automatically score leads, integrates with LinkedIn for prospect intelligence, and only passes on leads that are ready to buy right away will help in certifying quality leads before they are transferred onto sales.

An SLA also functions in the opposite direction, with the sales team routinely providing the marketing team with information on which leads were successful so they can produce more of them.

Give the marketing team a daily report on the status of the leads they forward. Make the report simple to read. If they know you are contacting them, they'll send you additional leads. Also, they'll provide you with the top leads. The marketing teams are in severe need of prompt follow-up and feedback on their leads. When they submit their month-end reports, they appear terrific. Along with the marketing team, decide on a timeline for regular feedback (SLA). They'll be astounded.

6. Involving numerous corporate decision-makers

Salespeople aim for ties within the organization to be three wide and three deep. This means that a salesman should have at least three contacts at the top of the organization, and these relationships should be able to create inroads within the company three levels deep, toward the important decision-makers.

selling to decision makers: Salespeople are finding it more and more difficult to influence multiple decision-makers and influencers, but this problem can be solved by developing helpful content that is aimed at the organization and the different personas within it (decision-makers and influencers), which then becomes readily shareable among colleagues.

Solution: Do you recall the query that is frequently posed to you? Now, expand it, print it on letterhead, and label it "Special Report."

Add two additional parts. One for the influencers and one for the decision-makers (perhaps the CEO, CFO, Head of XYZ, etc). (maybe the IT manager, administrator, or accountant...).

In your response, describe the situation as you would if you were actually in front of that character. Send your contacts at the prospect a PDF of this document. I wrote this with the idea that it might help you with your decision-making. If it performs well, request that the marketing division turn it into an official sales document with your brand on it.

7. Steer clear of discounts
No company wants to get involved in a price war because it invariably results in a race to the bottom and no one wins. Salespeople might think of haggling over prices to attract new

clients, but in the end, this becomes a client expectation and there is no backtracking.

DiscountSales representatives should think about adding value rather than making price concessions as a way to reach an understanding with potential customers.

Solution: By including the Document above in the sales process, you've created value. Find something you can deliver at a very low cost right now. It must be something the customer will find extremely useful and something your competitors either won't think to include in the bargain or just can't. When we are finalizing a new CRM deal, I frequently toss in SEO analysis. My customers adore this.

8. Phone communication (getting in touch)
How is it that even though we now cannot imagine living without our mobile devices, salespeople continue to struggle to connect with

customers over the phone? It is true that with so many ways to communicate, people frequently prefer email or text conversations to phone calls. Individuals are also harder to contact due to their hectic schedules.

1st sales call Other forms of communication that don't require two individuals to be present at once can be considered by salespeople. Yet, I continue to believe that phone conversations are crucial to the sales process. There is a lot that is discussed between a call's objective. There are so many small indicators that can increase your deal chances.

Solution: You may call a prospect when they open your email or quote by using software like HubSpot CRM to tag your emails. Given that you aren't interfering with another activity, meeting, or procedure, they will very certainly respond. This increases the relevance of connecting. Also, if a transaction fails and they view your quotation six months later, you still have a live one.

9. Making use of social media in the selling process

Understanding how to leverage social media platforms in the selling process is one of the biggest challenges facing sales representatives today. It all boils down to knowing where your leads are and communicating with them through the channels they like.

Social marketing While determining the greatest match for business tactics to interact with their audience, sales should collaborate with the marketing teams to understand where clients are disseminating online. The best prospects can then be found and targeted using suitable social media platforms like the business-to-business network LinkedIn.

Solution: Sponsored LinkedIn InMail campaigns are a very effective technique for focusing on brand-new prospects in extremely niche markets. Even if it takes a bit more time, one-on-one InMails are a fantastic alternative if you lack the technical know-how or the marketing team to execute on this.

10. CRM tools

CRMs are frequently solely perceived by sales teams as additional administration that slows them down and offers few advantages. That is not the situation. CRMs are made to support sales representatives in their work and cut down on administrative tasks so they have more time to speak with prospects.

Solution: The CRM must be correctly implemented and tailored to the needs of the sales representatives who will use it and the procedures they adhere to. If implemented properly, a CRM will be a priceless tool that helps sales representatives manage and close more leads and deals.

11. Making a point of urgency

Prospects purchase on their own schedules, which conflicts with the sales team's goals and the urgency they feel to seal deals.

Solution: You can encourage your prospects to sign by setting a deal value deadline or outlining the time needed to implement their product.

12. Addressing concerns about the price

Prospects can be given the price in two ways: simply by seeing it on your website, or by having a thorough conversation with them. When the prospect is comparing your pricing to that of your competitors or when their perceived value is low, the latter gets complicated.

Solution: Increase the prospect's perceived value to the value they will actually receive for that price. If you address their genuine problem, the value will be clear. Are they being pressured to buy something just because they indicated an interest in it, or do they actually need the service or product?

Understanding your competitors and the market price is essential. Do you charge too much or is the worth and caliber of what you provide greater? If you want to boost sales through upsells and repeat business, do you need to cut your prices to make fundamental goods and services valuable?

13. Chief oversight
Depending on how effectively ongoing marketing activities operate, sales teams may quickly get overwhelmed with leads at all stages of the buyer's journey.

Solution: Leads can be segmented using a CRM based on where they are in the purchasing process. So that sales teams only work with prospects who are prepared to be engaged, marketing can then qualify leads. Using a CRM, a process can be established to qualify leads and prospects, nurture them, and get in touch with them as needed.

14. Potential Leads

Focusing on the right prospects who enter the funnel at the right times is essential since it costs money for sales teams to waste time on unqualified leads.

Reliable lead selection criteria for sales and marketing must be used in an effective sales enablement approach.

Solution: If your company has the right personas in place, you can easily consult them while assessing prospective clients.

You can categorize the standards you apply to evaluate potential clients into the following groups:

Is the customer a good fit for one of your established personas?
They demand the needs of their potential customers, and whether and how your solution may meet those needs.
The method used to make decisions: Who is the main buyer in this transaction, and how many people are involved?
Your competitors are How many competitors do you have, and how do your products differ from those of your competitors?
Do they conduct business in the region you've chosen as your target market?

15. Providing for leads when they require it

While it is simple to call and email a list of potential clients, the first interaction you have with them could make or break a relationship. Analysis of each prospect requires a lot of time and has many gaps if there is insufficient activity tracking.

Solution: Sales teams can set up reminders in a CRM for themselves to analyze a prospect once certain events take place. Moreover, actions could initiate automation that sends prospects emails at predetermined intervals. These actions can include everything from visits to specific pages on your website to opens and clicks on emails you send out automatically and as outreach.

The way we communicate can either make or break a sale. Of course, an effective salesperson should recognize that listening is considerably more crucial than speaking, yet it makes sense that speaking skills are crucial throughout a sales conversation.

CHAPTER 3

Maximizing The Effectiveness Of Your Voice In Sales

We communicate in a way that can either make or destroy a sale, yet so few of us actually put this into practice. I've worked with sales coaching customers who are smarter than I am, are extremely knowledgeable about the sales cycle, and are passionate about selling but still find it difficult to close deals. Sometimes this is down to the voice and how they use yours.

Five Techniques For Using Your Voice To Boost
Sales:

• Travel With Your Prospect

Few activities are as boring as taking a fast car,
riding a fast roller coaster, or listening to
rapid-paced music. The same applies to how you
sound. Your likelihood of enticing your prospect
to join you on that conversational journey
increases with the speed of your speech. By
speaking more quickly and utilizing faster
words, you can amplify the excitement of your
voice and the desire for what you are saying.

• Apply the brakes

The most crucial portion of a sales conversation
is when you ask for the sale. Certainly, you can

pitch, list all the advantages, and walk the prospect through the pricing strategy, but if you don't ask for the sale, you will hardly ever close a deal. Some people actually accelerate up at this point because they are nervous, but this just adds to your overall enthusiasm.

At this stage you want to slow down on the words that need emphasizing which will help to highlight the point you are trying to make. The change in tempo will also ensure that the prospects attention is regained, and they too can start to allow decisions to be made.

• Monitor Volume

Nobody enjoys being talked to. And raising one's voice is disliked by everyone. Yes, making a loud statement might draw attention and emphasize a point, but occasionally this can come across as too harsh for the finer nuances to be heard. The goal is to almost whisper particular elements of your sales pitch that you feel need to be highlighted. This is a terrific approach. By whispering, we draw the potential client closer, forcing them to pay attention both physically and cognitively. The potential client will pay closer attention to make sure they get what you are saying. Also, you'll convey the idea that you are sharing a secret with them that only they should know. This will aid in building a solid rapport with your potential client and draw them in for the most crucial sections of your pitch.

•Quit talking.

As we previously discussed, many of us tend to become over excited when asking for a sale and even talk ourselves out of making the request. Have you ever presented a product or service to someone, asked for the sale, and then felt the need to defend your price or reiterate your case for why the customer should choose you? This is a major sales no-no. By doing this, you gain control of your prospects' thinking. You have to re-ask for the sale once you stop them from making a decision and start a new conversation. You have come full circle.

The next time you close a deal or finish your pitch, just be silent. You might initially feel a little strange doing it because it can be really difficult, but once you master it, your sales will soar. Thus, you anticipate hearing:

Well, Mrs. Prospect, that will cost you £140 if you enroll right away.
•Keep quiet.

Wait for your potential customer to talk. The prospect will once again have the choice to accept and will have the opportunity to ask additional questions or raise concerns as necessary.

•Breathe

Our voices are potent instruments. Yet, our breath is the real source of strength behind our speech. Correct breathing will help us apply the aforementioned voice techniques, will relieve stress, and will allow us to maintain total control over the sales talk.

People make snap judgments about you when you speak, even though they don't know you. The more influence you have on those people and what you want them to do, the quicker you may gain control over those first perceptions.

You might influence people positively, annoy them negatively, or even intimidate them depending on your message. Nevertheless, speaking is not your only means of communication. Regardless of the words you use, dominance, authority, and controlling someone's attention have a deeper and more potent effect.

Your voice and its acoustic characteristics serve as that potent weapon.

Slow down and speak in a strong, authoritative voice.

One of my closest friends can foresee upcoming movie plot twists with startling precision. Up until the day she disclosed her "secret," I was constantly in awe of her brilliance. Most of us are too engrossed in the movie to give the music any thought, but if you do, you may also anticipate what is about to happen. Much as how we use our voices, directors also employ the musical score. The issue is that we won't be able to forecast how our message will be received unless we are paying attention to what our voices are saying. We should be able to do it with surprising accuracy, as my friend so aptly noted.

Your voice is the most effective instrument for conveying assurance and confidence in sales scenarios. How carefully do you listen to your voice? not the words you use, but how you do it. The majority of you will likely respond "not at all," which may be holding you back from reaching greater success.

People will want to listen to you if they enjoy the sound of your voice. While in a sales position, go more slowly. When making a sales presentation, you shouldn't use the word "rapid talker," which has a bad connotation. Many people speak more quickly when they're excited. Your potential customers perceive you as trying to trick them psychologically. Speed up. Match your prospect's voice tempo, manner, and pitch by listening to how they speak.

"A voice is a gift given to humans; it should be valued and used to produce communication that is as human as possible. Silence and helplessness go together. Atwood, Margaret
You may use your voice as a potent instrument to help you succeed in business. Everyone has a voice, but not everyone uses it to build rapport with clients, persuade others, or control initial impressions. One-third of the overall impression you leave on others comes from your voice (remember your appearance and the message you deliver are the other two-thirds).

Even if you appear and act with the utmost confidence, your voice will instantly show any fear, anxiety, anger, boredom, or bewilderment unless you know how to manipulate it. You should be able to vocally convey yourself clearly and talk in a range that sounds both natural and appealing. You want to sound kind and approachable when speaking. You should also come across as vigilant and motivated.

Although you need a voice that can be heard, going above and beyond is needless for your prospect and physically hazardous for you. The nearly unconscious tightening of the neck muscles to force sound out is a frequent outcome of striving too hard. In addition to strain, hoarseness, and painful throat, this results in unclear speech, which is the worst possible outcome. Ease can be attained by maintaining good posture, breathing properly, adjusting your jaw and throat muscles correctly, and being confident.

You need to have control over how loudly or softly, quickly or slowly, you speak to be an effective speaker at any level, whether it's at a prospect's home or a presentation with multiple attendees. Start becoming more conscious of your voice loudness, speaking rate, and tone today.

CHAPTER 4

More Sales Does Not Ensure More Profit

Many people in business either think that increasing sales will increase profits or who want you to think that increasing sales will increase profits. Let me say this: Increasing sales does not increase profit.

Sales are crucial, and I'm not in the least bit implying that they aren't. Sales are only one aspect of a firm, though. If used properly, it can be a significant asset; nevertheless, if allowed to continue selling nonstop, it might ruin your company. To build sustainable sales revenue and sustainable profit, it is crucial to comprehend how it can do that as well as what may be done to stop it.

Let's start with the fundamentals: sales representatives who are actively courting as many clients as they can in the hopes of spurring more quote requests and, ultimately, more sales, are doing more harm than good to your company. They adhere to the dated notion that increased activity equates to increased sales. Sure, more sales result in more income, but should your sales team's primary goal be to increase revenue?

The answer is straightforward: being busy does not provide the intended outcomes. Your salespeople are busy if they are frantically circling their areas, chatting with people, meeting new individuals, and so on. This activity will lead to quote activity, which will lead to revenue. It won't make any money. The goal of the company is profit, not sales.

What then will you do about it?
Starting with the product you are selling. You might offer a wide range of goods or services. Some are more profitable for a variety of

reasons, while others are simpler to sell for a variety of factors. Selling the appropriate goods or services in the appropriate quantities is the key. In other words, sell the things that bring in the most cash—in this case, profit—for you. I'll give you an illustration:

CHANGE YOUR SALES FORCE'S PRIORITY FROM REVENUE TO PROFIT

I was employed by a business that offered home health care. We had a healthy profit margin of roughly 42% on our regular services. We provided a specific service that amounted to little more than being the client's companion or sitter. They did not provide any form of care, including guidance or direct treatment. Since the services were needed for ailing parents and disabled family members, this organization was well-liked by the wealthy market. Short version: With gross earnings averaging over 75%, that specific category was extremely profitable for us. Some members of our sales team opposed to offering this kind of service and preferred to market more glitzy healthcare options with higher commissions per sale. That didn't increase our financial success. More sales undoubtedly increased our revenues, but profitability did not increase as a result. We changed the way we compensated salespeople by offering better awards for more profitable sales and lower prices for less profitable sales. Our sales team's emphasis shifted from revenue to profit.

Sales are frequently viewed as a business's growth indicator. In some ways, it is, but a completely different standard serves as the ultimate gauge.

Be extremely explicit with me.

Sales revenue is only a benchmark and has no direct bearing on how well your company is doing.

Even in the example I just gave, a company's success cannot be predicted just by its concentration on profitability. Focusing on the factors that lead to the excellent delivery of your goods or services is the key to success, especially lasting success. It entails being effective and encouraging an environment that is effective (and yes that culture drives your sales strategy too) Being effective requires the control of:

Whether they like it or not, every business creates waste. Waste is a natural byproduct of manufacturing, including materials that are the wrong size and typical byproducts.
Continuous Workflow - Your efficiency and cost will be affected by how your process is carried out step by step.
Idle Time - An employee who is waiting for another employee is either working unpaid time

or receiving compensation for that period. A loss has occurred.

Delivery costs apply to both delivering your goods and services to customers as well as getting your supplies to you.

Problem-solving skills are essential for finding a rapid and effective solution to a challenge using a superior method, substance, or item.

There are numerous approaches to dealing with those 5 areas, and each one demands work and dedication. Once you do, not only will your sales be more successful, but what you sell will also be delivered and offered more successfully, leading to sustained development. It is a gauge of a successful business.

The fact that too many business owners don't completely understand their sales is one of my pet peeves when I visit companies right now. I refer to these people as "busy fools" since too many are working away, earning sales, without fully considering the profits they're producing.

A busy fool is, for instance, a vacation rental company that has managed to raise occupancy rates while lowering costs and, consequently, revenue. They frequently grumble, "Our bookings are up on last year, why are we still struggling," when I visit a company like that. and they haven't considered the fact that they have so drastically lowered their offer that they haven't benefited financially from the additional occupancy.

Do the math.

Without strict control over your numbers, it's simple to discover that a company is actually offering more of something overall for less money than it did previously. Even though it seems straightforward, it's remarkable how many companies make this mistake. To find out where your most profitable locations are, you must

regularly evaluate your sales numbers and analyze trends.

I work with a technological company that sells a variety of goods, and together we started closely analyzing each sale that came in so that they could identify the most lucrative ones and invest their money there. As a result of doing that, we have come to understand that their solutions-based products are vastly more profitable than the hardware they offer. We have now implemented a strategy that is focused entirely on increasing the number of sales leads for solutions so that they can benefit from the high-profit margins there. This company now

has a clear plan for the upcoming year and a growth sector to focus on.
Search within yourself for solutions.

To understand your business properly, you need to know what kind of sales leads you to need, what kind of conversion rate you get from those leads, the average profit per sale, and how long it actually takes to get that money in. I tell every company I work with this, and I would say to any business reading this. It will provide you with a comprehensive sales approach if you comprehend and are aware of all of those items. It's incredible how few businesses have comprehensive responses to each of those questions.

Another thing I'd add is that I graduated from high school with a math grade of E, so it's not something that takes a degree in economics to be accurate. You only need to capture and then keep track of these numbers because they are all present in your company. You will receive responses by doing that, albeit they might not always be what you were hoping for. You'll be able to discover where your firm is actually profitable and which sections are not.

CHAPTER 5

The World Of Business Combines Elements Of Both Art And Science.

Creativity is essential to business. It's like painting. You begin with a completely blank canvas. You can paint anything and everything, which is exactly where your first challenge lies. There are a billion awful paintings just screaming to drip from your brush, and for every wonderful picture that you might turn out, there are a thousand more that you might turn out. Even works that are not successful are valuable, which is one of the most fundamental and challenging truths for an artist to learn. The creative manifestation of one's expertise is what we refer to as art. The very act of creating art is an attempt to create order out of disorder.

Observation and experimentation form the basis of the scientific method, which is a way to collect knowledge known as intellectual study. A famous quote attributed to Albert Einstein states that "research" would not exist if scientists knew what they were doing. Businesses are aware of the benefits that big data and analytics may provide for their operations. The overwhelming amount of data that we have access to needs to be analyzed to gain insights that will lead to improved judgments and more smart business moves. Experimentation based on newly acquired knowledge is also a crucial component. This is done so that we can observe what happens when a company tries something new. For example, we want to determine whether the increased number of units sold was due to the marketing campaign or whether the increased number of returning customers was due to the increased availability of customer support. The application of carefully gathered data and empirical evidence to solve problems is the essence of scientific inquiry.

The acquisition of knowledge is the domain of science, whereas the application of that knowledge is the province of the arts. It is possible to define art as any action that calls for the application of a skill, and as is common knowledge, managing a company calls for the use of a wide variety of skills.

Entrepreneurs strive to turn their visions into reality, while innovators come up with fresh concepts in the same way that artists express their imaginations through their work. The imagination must be inspired by something, and with easy access to the internet and all the data that is available there, as well as social media and how simple it is to be informed by other people from across the world, it is not difficult to find inspiration. It is simply a matter of working through the confusion caused by the data and putting order to it via the use of analytics and observation.

The combination of art and science is a never-ending circle in business. Data analysis stimulates the imagination to produce something novel, followed by testing of the concept to determine how well it performs in the marketplace and whether or not it should be implemented. In a never-ending effort to strike a balance between art and science, it continues with the process of acquiring information, creating from it, and experimenting with it.

Finding a Happy Medium Between Art and Science in Business

The majority of people consider business to be a science. Math and strategy are both required here. Those who pursue business studies at the university level can earn a Bachelor of Science or a Master of Science degree. But, when it comes to actual practice, business is a combination of art and science. The science behind your company guarantees that it functions efficiently, but the art behind it is what sets it apart from competitors and compels people to keep coming back for more. The key to achieving success is striking a balance between these two aspects so that they may collaborate to produce a sustainable model.

The Field of Study

The numbers are really where it's at when it comes to the science of business. The entirety of your company's past can be condensed into a single paragraph by reading your financial statements and analytical reports. You can view both your highs and lows, determine which techniques were successful, and then utilize this information to make plausible forecasts about the future.

In the end, determining whether or not you are making any money is the central focus of the scientific study of business. The flow of money is the engine that drives your company forward. A profitable and long-lasting enterprise is impossible to maintain in its absence. Tracking your progress and developing a strategy for sustained achievement into the future is made possible when you make use of measures like profit margin, cost of goods sold, fixed expenses, and return on investment.

The Artwork

As people, we are all unique. We are all unique in terms of the skills we have, the characteristics that make up our personalities, and the things that fascinate us. This one-of-a-kind trait is enthusiastically embraced by the art of running a business. The capability of a company to differentiate itself in the market is one of the most important factors in its level of commercial success. Your company is a direct reflection of all the intricacies that make you stand out as a unique individual if you are the owner of a business. For this reason, it is crucial for you to first identify your own innate strengths, interests, and ambitions so that you may use these to produce a higher value for the audience that you are aiming to attract.

Your capacity for original thought is another essential component of being successful in business. Many people are under the impression that they do not belong to the creative class. On the other hand, in the same way that anyone may launch their own company, anyone can think creatively. Your ability to think creatively will allow you to devise fresh strategies for communicating and marketing your company, as well as uncover new avenues for expansion.

When you mix the individuality of both your company and yourself with your capacity for creative thought, you may

connect with your clientele on a level that is far more profound than before. This authentic form of engaging with customers raises awareness, creates positive interaction, and ultimately results in long-term brand loyalty. Most importantly, it demonstrates that you care about what you do, which will ultimately result in your customers caring about both you and your company.

The Science

Business economics is actually all about statistics. Your financial accounts and analytical reports can provide an overview of your company's complete history. You may analyze your highs and lows, determine which tactics were effective, and utilize this data to predict the future with reasonable certainty.

The science of business ultimately revolves around determining whether or not you are making any money. The fuel that keeps your business functioning is money. You cannot run a sustainable business without it. Metrics like profit margin, cost of goods sold, fixed expenses, and return on investment can

be used to track development and develop a strategy for future success.

The Right Amount

The most successful business owners are those who understand that the art of being who they are translates into touching customers in ways that reinforce the value of what is being offered and that provide a positive emotional connection.

In other words, they know that touching customers in this way is the key to their own success. They are also aware of the significance of the science of business, which needs the efficient application of

business systems to boost both operational efficiency and profitability.

Individuals can develop a business model that is not only original but also viable if they strike a balance between the art and science of running a firm.

CHAPTER 6

Taking Your Business To The Next Level

When it comes to running a business, feeling stuck is not an uncommon experience for owners. You can feel that you're in a rut because your sales have plateaued, it's become difficult to recruit personnel to staff up, or both of these things might be true. When something like this occurs, you can require a fresh pair of eyes to assist you in locating approaches to reinvigorate and expand your company.

Your neighborhood Small Business Development Center (SBDC) is an excellent resource to utilize because it provides free counseling, in addition to the training that is frequently offered at no cost or at a very cheap cost. SBDCs collaborate with a wide variety of owners of small businesses and can identify opportunities where you may only perceive roadblocks.

1. Communicate with your customers through a variety of channels.

If you are a retailer who does not currently have an online presence, opening a web store could be an additional option for you to make sales. When you have collected a sufficient number of consumer emails, you should think about launching an email marketing campaign to keep your message in front of your client base. Also, keep in mind the importance of social media.

If you own a business that is solely accessible online, you might want to try running a direct mail campaign that includes a catalog showcasing your most popular items to attract new customers. After putting a multichannel strategy through its paces, you will be able to ascertain the most efficient use of your marketing budget by analyzing which channels contributed the most to the accomplishment of your sales objectives.

2. Look for staff members that are eager for a second shot.

We frequently hear that companies wish to expand to new levels but are unable to do so due to a shortage of available labor. Investigate opportunities such as working with "justice related" folks, who frequently have some training and/or certification as a result of their time spent incarcerated. They anticipate being offered entry-level positions, are anxious to find employment, and may have additional motivation to "show up and deliver" since they are required to report to probation or parole authorities. There may be additional financial benefits, such as tax credits, available to firms that hire these persons, and there are help programs available to further the professional growth of these new employees.

3. Adopt a time management strategy based on the 60/20/20 rule.

I recommend taking a more strategic approach to time management as opposed to the "Whack-a-Mole" strategy, in which you spend all of your time trying to finish as many jobs as possible as quickly as possible. First, you should allocate sixty percent of your time to proactively focus on projects that really provide value to your company or that others simply cannot do. The remaining forty percent of your time should be split between two activities: twenty percent should be spent planning, and the remaining twenty percent should be spent strategizing. When you spend time planning, you are allocating that time to the resources and schedules necessary for the operation of the business. When you spend time strategizing, you are allocating that time to evaluating how you can improve the performance of your business.

4. Go deep into your numbers

You really ought to be utilizing some kind of accounting software now that you run an established company. What else is there to measure if you have a foundational understanding? Learn the average number of times your inventory is sold each year and investigate your company's cash flow. Now is the moment to begin measuring your company's performance and making strategic use of metrics to advance your company to the next level.

5. Put in place and make use of several effective safety precautions.

It is not enough for businesses to simply be prepared for the next threat; rather, they need to prepare and enhance their cyberinfrastructure to position their firms to capitalize on the opportunities presented by a strong information security posture. Being prepared for the next threat is not enough for businesses; being prepared is not enough. The overwhelming cascade of messages communicated to owners of small businesses emphasizes the ongoing threat that malicious software and cybercriminal elements pose to the security of their digital information. This threat is exacerbated by the fact that malicious software and cybercriminal elements are constantly evolving. Because of the recent WannaCry ransomware assault, this danger has come to light for the first time.

The information security infrastructure of businesses needs to be reinforced as quickly as feasible so that it can be positioned and enhanced to meet the criteria that are required from larger corporate and government entities. This is something that needs to be done as soon as possible. The time has come for companies to set ambitious goals for themselves to improve their information security infrastructure. Consider your company's investment in information security less of a precaution against potential risks and more of a long-term strategy for the success of your business in the digital economy.

6. Make astute purchases of property and other assets.

Your business has the potential to grow if you can keep costs under control while generating profits. The more small businesses that provide ancillary services that you buy from, the more control you have over the costs of your major business, and the more clients and customers you obtain from the businesses that supply those services as a result of your purchases from those small businesses.

This is in addition to the fact that you can expand into new sectors of business or industries that were not previously handled by you, with the support of a partner that they already know and trust.

7. Build a business equipment chest.

A well-stocked business toolbox is a benefit to any corporation. In the toolset of your organization, you should have:

A business strategy to keep you on track with business success to avoid delays
A marketing plan that can offer your organization a presence in the industry and establish a loyal client base
An employee manual helps keep an informed workforce, defining rules and regulations and ensuring your organization complies with labor laws
Accounting software that can produce current financial reports at the push of a button, to keep track of all business operations

8. Stop using social media the wrong way

Companies need to quit the unhealthy habit of continually selling on social media. Marketing and sales are two distinct things and a sales-only approach on social media might as well be a fail-only strategy. Develop and document

content that delivers value to your audience and establishes a relationship with them. These might include industry insights, tips, and tricks, or even entertaining behind-the-scenes footage. Giving more than you take is the core of all relationships. Give out your knowledge, your industry trends, and your insights. That way when it comes time for a potential customer to make a purchase, they can turn to a brand they both know and trust

9. Attract the next generation of workers

There are a lot of organizations that are not fully prepared to hire the younger workforce that is available today. You need to make preparations in advance, find out about the possible strengths and weaknesses of the age group, and then rewrite your interview questions so that they put the best possible emphasis on the talent you are wanting to acquire.

It is essential to acquire the skills necessary to communicate with employees in a manner that enables them to comprehend the significance of their roles, duties, and positions within your company.

10. Plan for periods of inactivity

In farming, downtime is provided by Mother Nature; but, in other types of businesses, it is the responsibility of the entrepreneur to create their own downtime. This is not a time for vacation or "off-the-clock" work. This is time away from working in the business that is dedicated to working on the business, such as reviewing data, streamlining systems, and planning for the following day, week, quarter, or year, depending on the timeframe that makes the most sense for your company. Even if you can only set aside an hour, this will provide you the opportunity to formulate a plan of action and gain valuable insight into

potential concerns before they become significant problems.

11.. Act like you know everything there is to know
Learn your numbers, such as your gross margin, your net profit, your credit ratings, the number of days cash on hand, and so on, so that you are always aware of the financial state of your company. Also, have a thorough understanding of your clientele, including who they are, where they can be found, and the steps that must be taken to win their business and keep it.

12. Establish a board of advisors

When it comes to improving the performance of your company, one of the most effective steps you can do is to establish an advisory board. An advisory board that is tailored to the challenges and opportunities that your company is currently facing is a powerful management tool that can provide access to industry professionals at little to no additional cost, provide you with new ideas, and assist you in running your company more effectively. You should carefully select a small team to participate in quarterly meetings with you to discuss concerns, develop a strategic plan, and regularly evaluate your progress. Having an advisory board can raise the value of your company, speed up the rate of your company's growth, and give you mentors that will help you stay focused on accomplishing your business goals.

13. Don't fall into a frequent tax trap
If you are seeking to reduce your taxable income, you should avoid making key business choices. You shouldn't run your company to beat

the government at its own game; rather, you should focus on turning a profit.

14. Ask and share

Never be afraid to ask questions of other business owners out of fear that you will appear to be less knowledgeable than you actually are. You are not the expert; rather, you are the business owner! A willingness to share one's business expertise is essential. It is through the sharing of knowledge that others will gain an impression of your self-assurance in constructing a firm, and it is also through this process that new collaborations will be found.

Planning for your company's future leadership is the only thing that can take it to the next level in terms of success. The silver tsunami of baby boomer business owners (who control more than half of all small business assets) suggests that a conversion to employee ownership as an ESOP or worker cooperative should be considered now, more than ever, and for the next decade.

Your legacy will be preserved if you make the transition to employee ownership since it will ensure that your company continues to operate and will provide buyers who are willing and able as well as those who know your company the best. In addition to this, it ensures that your employees have something to do while also providing them with assets in the form of ownership equity, which helps to maintain the stability of a community through the maintenance of jobs and taxes. In August of 2018, the federal government passed the Main Street Employee Ownership Act, which mandates outreach and technical assistance from SBDC staff to advise for employee-ownership transitions. Additionally, the SBA will expand loan access to employee-owned businesses as a result of this legislation's passage.

15. Create a comprehensive long-term plan

Create a plan that will assist you in achieving
your short-term goals, such as those that are
quarterly, semiannually, or annually based, and
develop your goals. Ensure that your strategy
takes into account the potential resources that
you will require, including cash, personnel,
equipment, inventory, and other running costs,
and ensure that the end result will be a service or
product that clients are interested in purchasing.
Determine the metrics that you will use to track
your progress toward achieving that goal, and
make any necessary adjustments to your plans
based on how close or far you are from
achieving your objective. Determine the reasons
why you are not meeting your goal if you are not
already doing so: Is it a matter of insufficient
resources? Is marketing not working? Are you
focusing on the appropriate subset of your
potential customers?

16. Statistics don't lie

Finding anomalies in costs and revenues is essential to refine profitability, and creating sound systems and processes is essential for doing so. You'll be able to figure out what's wrong much more quickly if you have point-of-sale (POS) systems, inventory management systems, and bookkeeping practices, processes, and procedures in place. In many cases, it is simple for business owners who have been operating their companies for a considerable amount of time to rely on qualitative data and, as a result, neglect

quantitative data that can be easily located. For instance, a retailer might have the impression that a particular item is selling like hotcakes, but after looking at the numbers, they might realize that this is not actually the case.

17. CFIMITYM

The world of business is obsessed with acronyms such as ROI, URL, EIN, SMART, and SWOT. But "Cash Flow Is More Important Than Your Mother" (abbreviated as "CFIMITYM") is the one that stands out as the most significant. One of the primary reasons for the failure of small businesses is a deficiency in available cash.

Your business will fail more quickly than it would for any other reason if your cash reserves are insufficient (also known as "running out of money"). You can't pay your bills. You won't be able to pay the bills.

Your company can turn a profit while still coming up short on cash. Cash is the amount of money that is currently in the checking account of the business, while profit is a concept that is used in accounting.

If you are unable to collect what is owed to you, even if you have assets such as inventory or accounts receivable, you will not have cash on hand. And if you don't have any cash on hand, your company is doomed to fail.